6/18

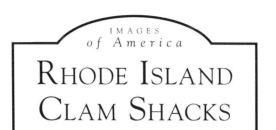

IMAGES
of America

RHODE ISLAND
CLAM SHACKS

D1562029

"O, clam, thou shalt not in a bake, with kindred bivalves nobly die; But shorn of former outward strength, chopped up within a fritter fry." This illustration, and the quotation, is from one of the earliest books about Rhode Island's clams, *Ye Tale of ye Clam*, an illustrated poem by John Henshaw and Henry B. Dearth, two Providence boys, published in 1883. (Providence Public Library.)

ON THE COVER: Dave's Seafood Restaurant was located at 719 Park Avenue in Island Park, Portsmouth, near Stone Bridge. The business seemingly survived Hurricanes Carol and Edna in 1954, but when Stone Bridge was closed permanently in 1956, the owners, World War I veteran David E. Lemay and his wife, Ida, relocated to Fall River. This photograph was taken about 1950. (Rhode Island State Archives.)

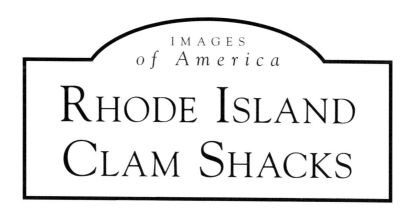

IMAGES
of America

RHODE ISLAND
CLAM SHACKS

Christopher Scott Martin and
David Norton Stone

ARCADIA
PUBLISHING

Published by Arcadia Publishing
Charleston, South Carolina

Printed in the United States of America

Library of Congress Control Number: 2016950047

For all general information, please contact Arcadia Publishing:
Telephone 843-853-2070
Fax 843-853-0044
E-mail sales@arcadiapublishing.com
For customer service and orders:
Toll-Free 1-888-313-2665

Visit us on the Internet at www.arcadiapublishing.com

To Kim, who helped with the research by ordering lots of lobster rolls, and to my parents, for, you know, raising me and stuff.

—Christopher

This book is dedicated to all those who treasure Rhode Island's clams; to my mother, Nancy, for feeding me well; and to Al and Joshua.

—David

CONTENTS

ACKNOWLEDGMENTS

We would like to thank all the individuals and institutions that shared images, ephemera, information, and reminiscences: Martha Ball; Jane Bitto of Evelyn's Nanaquaket Drive-In; Henry A.L. Brown; Ken Carlson at the Rhode Island State Archives; North Kingstown historian Tim Cranston; Elizabeth Donovan of the North Kingstown Free Library; Larry DePetrillo; Richard Donnelly and Van Edwards of the Barrington Preservation Society; Tammy Duhamel McLellan of the Hitching Post; Kevin Durfee of George's of Galilee; Steve Filippi of Ballard's Restaurant; Elsie Foy of Aunt Carrie's; Laurie Grann of the Crow's Nest Restaurant; Felicia Gardella of the Warwick Historical Society; Pam Gasner of the Block Island Historical Society; Charles Hall; Fred and Debbie Howarth of Finn's Seafood Restaurant and Ernie's Dockside Restaurant; Judy Wilcox Jencks; KarenLu LaPolice; Bob Larivee; Lisa Lepore; Carolyn Magnus of the Portsmouth Free Library; Amanda Maybeck of Champlin's Seafood Deck; Sandy McCaw; Louis McGowan of the Johnston Historical Society; Frederick Mikkelsen Jr.; Nancy Moore, Deb Ormerod, and Karen Panzarella of the East Providence Historical Society; Rachel Peirce; Deb Petrella of the Port Side Restaurant; James Rengigas of Gus's Restaurant and Mrs. Gus's; Riondo Ribeiro; Ed and Sandy Rice; Ed Serowick Sr.; Ray Simmons; the Tiverton Historical Society; Bob and Ingrid Trager of Skip's Dock; Keith Wahl; Marjorie Webster of the Portsmouth Historical Society; Kate Wells of the Providence Public Library; the New York Public Library; and Caitrin Cunningham and Samantha Langlois of Arcadia Publishing.

Images in this volume appear courtesy of the Providence Public Library (PPL), Christopher Scott Martin (CSM), and David Norton Stone (DNS), as well as others noted in individual courtesy lines.

INTRODUCTION

Rhode Island has always been renowned for clams and for luscious clambakes that cause the mouth to water with pleasurable anticipation. The earliest practitioners of clambakes ascribed Native American origins to the practice of steaming clams, corn, and fish over hot rocks and rockweed. Indeed, the shell middens of the Narragansett, Wampanoag, and Manisee tribes that have been discovered in coastal areas attest to the huge consumption of clams and other shellfish, long before Roger Williams, the founder of Rhode Island, arrived. In the 19th century, the clambake attained its greatest glory, thanks to the magnificent shore dinner halls that strove to outdo one another in size and entertainment, the steamboats vying to take people there, the price (50¢), and the abundance of steamer clams in Narragansett Bay. Rhode Island shore dinners became so famous that one hotel even painted its windows to advertise that it served them. That hotel was in Staten Island, New York.

The clambake is a ceremony, with each step of the process, from the heating of the rocks to the spreading of the tarp, evidencing skill and finesse. One bad clam could ruin a bake. Initially, clambakes were cooked and eaten outdoors, their rusticity part of the charm, and at one political bake in 1840 in Buttonwoods, men brought their own plates, bowls, spoons, knives, and forks and ate under the trees. Later, shore dinners were cooked outside but served at long tables in dining halls that emphasized water views over elegance and where the traditional fare of a clambake was supplemented by fish or clam chowder, clam cakes, lobsters, brown bread, ice cream, watermelon, and Indian pudding. Eventually, full-fledged amusement parks grew up around the most popular shore dinner destinations, like Rocky Point and Crescent Park.

The heyday of the clambake ended when the steamer clam nearly disappeared from Rhode Island waters, the victim of pollution and of the hurricane of 1938. The soft-shell clam had always been the preeminent symbol of Rhode Island, but over time a new clam, the quahog, was embraced on summer menus. As the automobile made the population more mobile, entrepreneurs like Carrie and Ulysses Cooper in Point Judith were opening clam shacks and restaurants, converting what had previously been inactive pasture land to magnets for those seeking recreation. The traditional clambake and shore dinner held on, but the quahog began to star in clam cakes and chowder, a combination that could be prepared and eaten much more quickly than the complete shore dinner.

Among the first clam shacks was Aunt Carrie's in Point Judith. Founded in 1920, it is the oldest continuously operating family-owned clam shack. It started as a shack and campground and later became a sit-down restaurant, modeled on a shore dinner hall. The current owner, Elsie Foy, has never changed the green and gold color scheme. Aunt Carrie is often credited (incorrectly but harmlessly) with having invented the clam cake. The story is that Aunt Carrie threw some chopped clams into her corn fritter batter when her children brought her some quahogs they had found. This was not the "eureka!" moment one might hope for. Clam fritter recipes were found in cookbooks published before Carrie Cooper's birth and had been served at Rocky Point's shore dinners as early as the 1860s. Growing up in nearby Wickford, surely Carrie had visited Rocky Point and sampled its fried balls of dough perfumed by clam juice and studded with clam morsels. What Carrie and her husband really invented was the clam shack itself, a place where clam cakes and chowder could stand alone as a meal, thanks largely to a unique clam cake recipe that, for nearly a century, has induced people to wait in line outside the shack's takeout windows.

The story of clams in Rhode Island is one of evolution, from clambakes to shore dinner halls to clam shacks and from the soft-shell clam to the quahog. The evolution story that historian Henry A.L. Brown tells of the Dolly Varden Tavern in Pawtuxet is truly unique. Before becoming a popular place for clambakes, it was reputed to have been a brothel. The Hummocks started as a clambake facility in the village of Hamilton, and after fires and hurricanes, its operator Henry Johnson opened a huge indestructible brick restaurant in Providence. George's, now one of the largest restaurants in the state, began as a simple lunchroom. Other places like Finn's on Block Island and Skip's Dock started as fish markets and still keep their hand in the fish-dealing trade.

The authors heard a lot of great stories talking to people who run clam shacks, about business and life. There is the woman who started working at her family's clam shack when she was five years old, standing on a Coca-Cola crate to see over the counter. Today, she continues the operation to honor her father and because of the uniqueness of owning such a historic business. There was the surprise of learning that Aunt Carrie's had doubled as a home for military officers during World War II. Our visits caused people to search through things they had perhaps never looked at before. One restaurant owner was pleased to find that her mother-in-law had kept a clipping of her wedding announcement. "I guess she was happy about it," she said modestly. There is the story of the man who earned his room and board on Block Island by painting the interior walls of a hotel, thus preserving what the old clam shacks and shore dinner halls looked like there.

While photographs may in some instances be scarce, sensory memories are not. Most Rhode Islanders of a certain age can recall exactly what Rocky Point chowder and clam cakes tasted like, and whenever a recipe appears online reputed to be "original," it is shared widely on social media, commented on profusely, and eventually fades away as it is recognized as just another imposter. At Rocky Point, Crescent Park, and the other high-volume places, the seafood owed its success not only to recipes, but to mass production techniques, like the clam cake dispenser that shot uniform balls of dough into the hot oil.

Today, Rhode Island's association with the clam is as secure as ever. Other states may have abandoned their regional cuisines, but the danger to shore dinner halls and clam shacks has never been falling out of fashion. Rather the threat is fire, wind, and water. The glory of Rhode Island's clam shacks and shore dinner halls—the way they are situated near or sometimes even over the water—has often been the cause of their destruction. Hurricanes and fires have claimed three Rocky Point shore dinner halls. Photographs, old menus, signs, and records disappear with these disasters. This book is an effort to preserve the history that remains.

At Rocky Point's shore dinner hall, the waiters let patrons know when it was time to make way for the next seating by sending one of the long rolls of paper that lined the table in the lingerers' direction. Here comes the paper now. Enjoy the clams.

One

CLAMBAKES

US senator and former Rhode Island governor Theodore Francis Green was the guest of honor at this 1947 clambake organized by the Kentish Guards. Standing in the background is Carlos, an East Greenwich restaurateur who always ran these bakes. The location might be Goddard Park in Warwick. (Frederick Mikkelsen Jr.)

Human use of Narragansett Bay's shellfish resources goes back many thousands of years, archaeological evidence of which includes shell middens like this replica example at the Block Island Historical Society. A midden is a trash heap, and it can reveal many things about the people who left it, like what they ate, how long they lived there, or what kinds of tools they used. Middens found in Rhode Island's coastal areas show that shellfish were very important to indigenous peoples' diet. In fact, it is believed Native Americans were actively managing oysters and quahogs long before Rhode Islanders ever got around to figuring out how to do it. (Block Island Historical Society; photograph by CSM.)

Eight men enjoy a clambake on the beach in this late-1800s stereo view. At its most fundamental level, the traditional clambake is unchanged from the days when Native Americans perfected it. (New York Public Library, Robert Dennis Collection.)

671 . Digging Clams at Camp Cole, R. I.

A successful clambake requires several things, not least of all some fresh clams. While today one would most likely buy them from a market or directly from a local quahogger, in days gone by, participants of smaller bakes might have collected them directly from nearby mudflats. This is a right that Rhode Islanders still hold today, but it is getting increasingly difficult for the casual clammer to access the shore. Camp Cole in Warwick was a popular getaway spot from the late 1800s to the 1960s. (Louis McGowan.)

Patience Island in Narragansett Bay was the setting for a clambake in July 1947. From left to right are Phillip Joseph Peckham Jr., Frederick W. Mikkelsen Sr., Phillip Joseph Peckham Sr., M. Schoos, G. Plouf, R. Farrell, unidentified, and G. Nelson. Behind Nelson is a pile of driftwood ready to be fired. (Frederick Mikkelsen Jr.)

A clambake can be a modest affair, like this small barrel bake, or a huge undertaking serving thousands of people, like the bake that took place at Buttonwoods in 1840 and reportedly fed between 8,000 and 10,000. (PPL.)

MEET ME AT KICKEMUIT GRANGE THURS. AUG. 20th, 1908.

For many decades, clambakes were the go-to outdoor activity for a wide range of people and for a wide range of reasons. Whether it was a family hosting a bake in their backyard, a social club at their own clubhouse, or an annual outing to reward employees for their hard work, the clambake was an experience to remember. This bake in Warren cost 50¢ in 1908! (Henry A.L. Brown.)

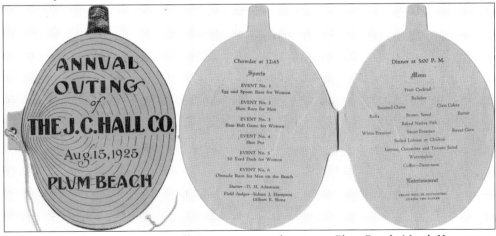

This 1925 invitation to the J.C. Hall Company annual outing at Plum Beach, North Kingstown, is more whimsical than most. The day began with chowder at 12:45 p.m., followed by various sporting activities. Dinner was at 5:00 p.m. and included steamed clams, clam cakes, brown bread, boiled lobster or chicken, and watermelon. The day concluded with coffee and entertainment. J.C. Hall was a commercial printer and lithographer in Providence. (KarenLu LaPolice.)

A group of railroad men pose on the occasion of their clambake on September 27, 1936. The location is unknown. Such an event at a time when the country was struggling to recover from the Depression must have been an especially welcome diversion. (Henry A.L. Brown.)

Clambakes at Tiverton's First Baptist Old Stone Church reportedly attracted as many as 1,500 attendees, sometimes including Rhode Island's governor and Providence's mayor. This postcard, dated 1912, shows what the parking situation looked like in the time of the Ford Model T. (Henry A.L. Brown.)

The "Rhode Island Clam Bake" was practically a brand name, recognized far and wide as a meal consisting of specific elements and served in a specific style. Melville Garden was a resort on Crow Point in Hingham, Massachusetts, that was active from 1871 to 1896. According to the 1888 *King's Handbook of Boston Harbor* by Moses Foster Sweetser, it featured a "clam-pavilion, where eight hundred persons can take their place at once, and partake of ship-loads of clams cooked in the genuine and unmodified manner of Rhode Island." The 1880 illustration above shows another way of playing with the visual possibilities of the clam. (Both, Henry A.L. Brown.)

MELVILLE GARDEN,

DWNER LANDING, . . . BOSTON HARBOR

OPEN EVERY DAY EXCEPT MONDAY.

One of the Finest Harbor Resorts in New England.

The Garden contains FIRST-CLASS RESTAURANT, BOWLING and SHOOTING ALLEYS, ILLIARD TABLES, PATENT SWINGS, FLYING HORSES, CAMERA OBSCURA, MENAGERIE, EAR PIT, &c. ROW BOATS and YACHTS to let.

RHODE ISLAND CLAM BAKE at 12, 4 and 6.30 o'clock. DINNER TICKETS, 50c.
EDMANDS' BAND, DAY AND EVENING.

e Garden will be Illuminated Every Evening with 20 Electric Light

Grand Concert by Edmands' Band Every Sunday Afternoon and Evening.

HINGHAM STEAMERS LEAVE ROWE'S WHARF at 5.45, 9 15, 10 30, 11 30, 12.30, 2.30, 3.30, 5.30, 30, 7.45 and *9.30. RETURNING, LEAVE DOWNER LANDING at 7, 7.35, 9.45, 10.35, 12.15, 1.15, 5.15, 6.45, †8.30, †9 30. CROSS TRIPS to and from NANTASKET BEACH. Leave Downer Land- g at 11.20, 12.20, 1.20 and 4.20. Leave Nantasket Beach at 9.30, 12, 1, and 4 50.
SUNDAYS. Boston to Downer Landing at 10.15, 2.15, 4.45, and 7.15. Downer Landing to Bos- n at 12, 3.30, 6, 9.30. †Mondays excepted. *Saturdays excepted.
BUY THE EXCURSION TICKET at Rowe's Wharf, 60 Cents. (OVER)

Every bake needs a bakemaster, an experienced person who assures that all the steps are followed in their proper order and at the proper time. Here, bakemaster Henry A.L. Brown waves to the camera as flames begin to consume the carefully constructed bake crib at the beginning of a bake at Salter's Grove in Pawtuxet in June 1983. It will be a few hours before the cooking part of the process can even begin. (Henry A.L. Brown.)

The bake begins early in the morning with a big fire constructed over specially selected rocks. Whether the bake is built in a pit or not depends on the bakemaster's preference and the location. Once the fire burns down to coals, the ash is raked away and the rocks may need to be repositioned to make an even bed, as the men with the long-handled rakes appear to be doing here. (PPL.)

The next step is to cover the hot rocks with rockweed. The moisture in the rockweed rapidly turns to steam, so workers must move quickly. Care must be taken to cover all the rocks completely, so that neither the food nor the tarp are burned. Note the spectator sport aspect of attending a bake, as a rapt crowd looks on. (PPL.)

All the ingredients of the bake go on top of the rockweed. Shellfish and vegetables can be piled up loose, in racks (as in this image), or half-barrels or cheesecloth bags. The bakemaster knows how to layer the ingredients to ensure all is cooked to perfection. This bakemaster, nearly enveloped in steam, has clearly chosen the wrong side of the bake from which to supervise. (PPL.)

Here, all the shellfish has been piled loose on the bake, although it appears it has been laid atop a net for easier removal later. Potatoes await their turn in the right foreground. (PPL.)

All the ingredients having been added, another layer of rockweed may be spread over the top. The whole bake is then covered with one or more canvas tarps. The tarp is carefully secured around the edges to keep as much steam inside as possible. The chimney in the background indicates that this bake may have taken place at the Hummocks in the mill village of Hamilton, in North Kingstown. (PPL.)

Participants cover the bake with canvas at the Gaspee Days clambake in Salter's Grove, Pawtuxet, on June 10, 1981. In the days before synthetic materials, old sail cloth would have been perfect for this purpose. The two men at left are Michael Cerrelli and Bob Sprague, and at right are John Laffey and Norman Habib. The others are unidentified. (Henry A.L. Brown.)

Now is the time for games, contests, and socializing. In some cases there may be appetizers—clam cakes (fried dough fritters studded with chopped clams) and chowder—to occupy participants while they wait. The bake will steam quietly away for the next few hours. (PPL.)

Clambake attendees play a spirited game of tug-o-war in this c. 1950 photograph. Other activities that might occupy eager diners, both women and men, included baseball, potato sack races, egg and spoon races, swimming, horseshoes, or even political speeches. (Larry DePetrillo.)

Finally it is time to uncover the bake. The tarp is drawn back, and the ingredients—clams, lobsters, corn, potatoes, and sausages—are quickly removed and served to eager bake-goers. (PPL.)

Johnson's Hummocks in North Kingstown was known in its time as clambake heaven. In 1905, Frank Johnson, who lived in the village of Hamilton, and his 16-year-old son Henry built the first permanent structure of the Hummocks on a sandy peninsula. It was nothing more than a roof resting on cedar posts, covering long benches and tables set on the bare ground. This was succeeded by a more formal pavilion in 1910, which in turn was extended into a dining hall with a capacity of 1,400. In 1925, a carelessly dropped cigarette started a fire that destroyed everything except the old Johnson family homestead. These photographs were taken in the 1910s by Wickford Village pharmacist E.E. Young. (Both, North Kingstown Free Library, Doc Young Collection.)

New England Automotive Jobbers
Outing at the Hummocks. Aug. 17. 1920.

Going on an outing in the country was no reason to leave one's tie at home. The employees of New England Automotive Jobbers still had to look presentable for their August 17, 1920, outing at the Hummocks. The two boxers at the front hint at one of the day's diversions, while what the

man at right is up to with a broom and a brick is anyone's guess. At one time, ball games, band concerts, and swimming, topped off with a good Johnson shore dinner, were part of the summer memories of many Rhode Island natives. (KarenLu LaPolice.)

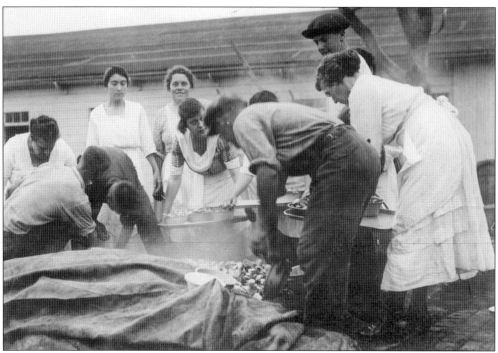

In August 1938, Henry Johnson rebuilt to carry on the tradition started by his father, but on September 21, "that big wind from the Caribbean came up and blew everything in the general direction of Providence," as noted in *It Started With A Clambake!*, a pamphlet by Johnson's Hummocks about its history. Although Johnson built again, a hurricane in 1944 blew the roof off the brand-new pavilion into the cove. Henry Johnson eventually established a disaster-proof brick restaurant farther up the bay on Allens Avenue in Providence. As shown in this photograph, in which clams are portioned out at the Hummocks, women were also enthusiastic participants in the bake process. (PPL.)

Longtime residents of Wesquage Beach recall that at the site of the current Twin Willows there was a restaurant and a general store where milk, bread, candy, and newspapers were sold. The mail was also delivered there. The building in this photograph around which picnickers have assembled may be that early restaurant. A clambake is under way at right. (PPL.)

24

Before the 1938 hurricane, high sand dunes extended along Wesquage Beach, as seen in this photograph from 1908. The development of nearby Bonnet Shores started in 1928, and by 1930, there were 12 houses on the land known as Wesquage Plat. (PPL.)

Here is a closer look at that cottage overlooking Wesquage Beach. No paper plates or plastic utensils are in use at this shack. The diners have made an impromptu table by laying planks across the porch railings. (PPL.)

This chapter concludes with another photograph from the July 1947 bake on Patience Island. After all the clams have been consumed, it is time to raise a final glass and maybe take a nap. From left to right are unidentified, Frederick W. Mikkelsen Sr., Eugene Plouff, two unidentified, George Nelson, and Philip J. Peckham Jr. (Frederick Mikkelsen Jr.)

Two

SHORE DINNER HALLS

Steamboats brought Rhode Island's shore resorts within reach of nearly everyone living in the state's industrialized communities, as attested by this 1894 map showing "all the Landing-places of the Continental Steamboat Co." Shown on the East Bay are Kettle Point, Squantum Point, Ocean Cottage, Silver Spring, Cedar Grove, Camp White, Portsmouth Grove, and Seaconnet Point. On the West Bay are Field's Point, Rocky Point, Oakland Beach, and Buttonwoods. Every resort and recreation area had its own pier, and most had a shore dinner hall or clambake pavilion. (PPL.)

One of many ferries that plied the waters of Narragansett Bay in the late 1800s and early 1900s, the *Vue De L'Eau* docked at South Water Street in Providence and made stops at Field's Point, Silver Spring, and Crescent Park. Note the name on the building at left. The Pettis family was in the oyster business from the 1840s to the first quarter of the 20th century. This photograph is from about 1888. (PPL.)

Established by the Rumford Chemical Works as a summer retreat for its workers, Hunt's Mills, in the East Providence village of Rumford, had a carousel, dance hall, vaudeville hall, picnic grounds, and canoeing on the Ten Mile River, but it never had a shore dinner hall. Instead, this café, built in commemoration of a Japanese diplomat's visit to the 1902 New England Association for Arts and Crafts Exposition at Crescent Park, greeted visitors at the park's landward entrance. (East Providence Historical Society.)

Here is another view of the Hunt's Mills Café around 1911. Note the Japanese influence in the curve of the roof. Hunt's Mills operated from the 1890s until 1923, when the dance hall burned down. Today, the John Hunt House (out of frame to the right of the café) is the headquarters of the East Providence Historical Society. The stone bridge can still be seen, but in place of the café there is a modern gazebo. (Ed Serowik Sr.)

The Squantum Club in East Providence traces its roots to informal clambakes, held since 1843 by two groups on Whortleberry (or Huckleberry) Island just to the south of Squantum Point. The groups—underclassmen from Providence High School and the Rowseville Boys, a circle of merchants and businessmen from South Water Street—joined together in 1868. This engraving is from about 1881. (CSM.)

The Squantum Club's main clubhouse, shown here in a c. 1907 postcard view, was built on Squantum Point in 1872. It replaced a simple open-framed pavilion that was erected the previous year. (CSM.)

This view of the Squantum Club's 1889 bakehouse comes from a c. 1910–1915 menu. The Squantum Association still operates the exclusive club today as a venue for weddings and corporate events. (Henry A.L. Brown.)

Located south of the Squantum Club, Ocean Cottage was opened by Peleg Sherman in 1863 on 20 acres. At first only reachable via a carriage road from Pawtucket Avenue, a wharf was later built across to Huckleberry Island allowing for ferry access. This engraving is from around 1881. (CSM.)

Later owned and expanded by C.J. Read, Ocean Cottage offered accommodations for 25 permanent boarders, and its shore dinner hall could seat 300 people at a time. An experiment was once made there using coiled steam pipes instead of hot rocks for a clambake. The clams were cooked properly but lacked the "savory flavor" of the traditional method, and the experiment was deemed a failure. (PPL.)

Boyden Heights was an amusement park opened by George B. Boyden in 1904 on the former grounds of Ocean Cottage. While it had many features in common with other resorts like Crescent Park and Rocky Point, it failed to capture the public's attention and was closed by 1910. Now the property is a suburban neighborhood; the bandstand (at right) is now a private residence. (Ed Serowik Sr.)

Almost adjoining Ocean Cottage, Silver Spring was opened in 1869 by Hiram D. Maxwell. It had its own steamship landing and bakery, and its dining hall, located on the rocky shore, could comfortably accommodate 600 people for shore dinners in a season that ran from June 1 to September 20. Silver Spring is depicted here in a c. 1881 engraving. (CSM.)

A June 13, 1883, blurb in the *Evening Bulletin* noted that "a large number availed themselves of the opening of the season and the consequent shore dinner at Silver Spring to-day. Every seat in the main dining hall was filled, and the dinner itself was excellent, including the succulent clam, baked and in chowder, blue fish, lobster, clam cakes, etc. etc., and not only was the dinner itself good, it was promptly served. It is a notable fact that Silver Spring clams are free from grit, by no means a small consideration to clam-eaters who have sensitive teeth." (PPL.)

Vanity Fair was to be George B. Boyden's masterpiece, and for a few years, it was truly grand. Inspired by the 1902 Pan-American Exposition in Buffalo, it centered around one major attraction—Chute the Chutes—with other attractions, shops, and concessions arranged around it. The park's shore dinner hall, called the College Inn, is the large building just off center. Between it and the pier is a separate clam bake house. (Ed Serowik Sr.)

Here is the midway of Vanity Fair around 1907, showing the fanciful architecture inspired by the Pan-American Exposition of 1902. A sign on the pavilion at center points the way to the shore dinner hall, the building with the arched colonnade at right. In the bandstand, the members of Fay's American Band almost outnumber the crowd for whom they are performing. (PPL.)

Another view of Vanity Fair's shore dinner hall is presented in a 1909 postcard. Vanity Fair opened in 1907 and only three years later was suffering from low attendance and financial woes. A fire in 1912 sealed the park's fate, and the property was purchased by Standard Oil. Today, Silver Spring Golf Course occupies the land. (Louis McGowan.)

The private Pomham Club in East Providence began in the late 1800s as a place for gentlemen to network over shore dinners of lobster, steamed clams, corn, and potatoes. It closed in 1954, and the property was redeveloped for condominiums in the 1980s. (CSM.)

Titled "Unexpected liberality," this cartoon by T.S. Sullivant from the July 1918 issue of *Browning's Monthly Magazine* is a satirical look at a common complaint: "Waiter, I don't wish to get the Proprietor into trouble, but I feel it my duty to inform the Food Controller of there being a clam in this chowder." (Henry A.L. Brown.)

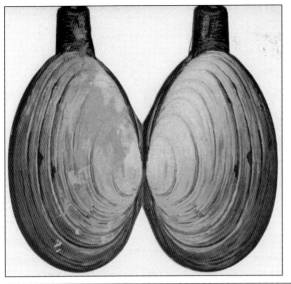

A typical spread at the Pomham Club is detailed in this invitation to the American Electrical Works' 22nd annual bake in 1900. Many items, like lobster salad, clam chowder, and clam cakes, are staples of clam shacks today. Others, like fried eels and stewed liver with wine sauce, not so much. Shore dinners nearly as generous as this were served at every shore dinner hall, and for many years, the price was just 50¢! The creative design of clambake invitations like this led to many being saved in scrapbooks. (Both, CSM.)

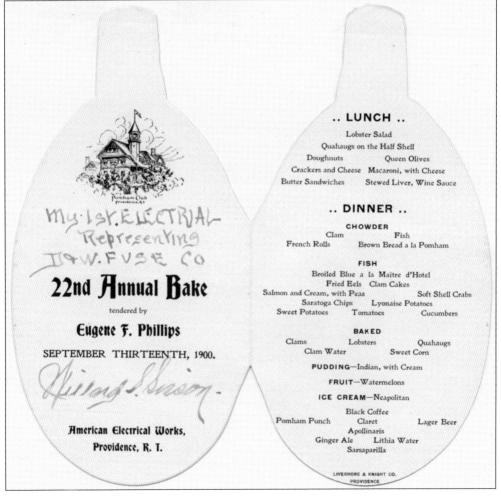

Pomham Club
Providence, R.I.

My 1st ELECTRICAL Representing I&W. FUSE CO

22nd Annual Bake

tendered by

Eugene F. Phillips

SEPTEMBER THIRTEENTH, 1900.

American Electrical Works,
Providence, R. I.

.. LUNCH ..

Lobster Salad
Quahaugs on the Half Shell
Doughnuts   Queen Olives
Crackers and Cheese Macaroni, with Cheese
Butter Sandwiches   Stewed Liver, Wine Sauce

.. DINNER ..

CHOWDER
Clam   Fish
French Rolls   Brown Bread a la Pomham

FISH
Broiled Blue a la Maitre d'Hotel
Fried Eels   Clam Cakes
Salmon and Cream, with Peas   Soft Shell Crabs
Saratoga Chips   Lyonaise Potatoes
Sweet Potatoes   Tomatoes   Cucumbers

BAKED
Clams   Lobsters   Quahaugs
Clam Water   Sweet Corn

PUDDING—Indian, with Cream

FRUIT—Watermelons

ICE CREAM—Neapolitan

Black Coffee
Pomham Punch   Claret   Lager Beer
Apollinaris
Ginger Ale   Lithia Water
Sarsaparilla

LIVERMORE & KNIGHT CO.
PROVIDENCE

Esmeralda Camp Ground, part of Camp White, is shown here in 1887. After he opened Ocean Cottage in 1863, Peleg Sherman established Camp White at a farmhouse in Riverside and served shore dinners there. The camp, located just north of Crescent Park, included acreage on both sides of Bullock's Point Avenue and remained in use until shortly before 1923. (Ed Serowik Sr.)

George B. Boyden opened Crescent Park, named for its crescent-shaped beach, in 1886, and this photograph dates from around that time. The "CAFE" to the left of the pier is an early version of the shore dinner hall. The Crescent Park Hotel can be seen through the trees to the right of the pier. (PPL.)

In its day, Crescent Park was called "The Coney Island of New England." Jacob Hoch was the chef at the park in 1894. (Ed Serowik Sr.)

A quahog riding a pig? It makes sense when Crescent Park, known for its clambakes, held a pig roast in February. The illustration comes from an unidentified 1901 newspaper. George B. Boyden sold the park the following year. (Henry A.L. Brown.)

The Crescent Park Shore Dining Hall was built around 1895. Searle's "Famous 6 O'clock Bake" cost 60¢–85¢ and ran from noon to 8:00 p.m. This photograph was taken sometime between 1905 and 1910. (Ed Serowik Sr.)

Another view of Crescent Park's shore dining hall dates from around 1906. The dining halls of all the shore resorts were built right next to their piers, so they were one of the first things visitors saw upon disembarking from the ferry. (Louis McGowan.)

This menu from the Crescent Park Shore Dining Hall dates from the 1920s, when John Clare was manager. Prices range from 65¢ for clam cakes and chowder to $1.90 for a full-on "Genuine Indian Style Clambake," including lobster, "Special Crescent Park Sausage," watermelon, and Indian pudding. The helpful elves around the border are collecting and preparing the ingredients. (Ed Serowik Sr.)

Ed Serowik Sr. found this discarded sign under the Crescent Park Carousel. It reads, in part, "Season of 1925. Announcing Lyon's Old Time Indian Style Famous R.I. Clam Bake Known all over the U.S.A, being served at Crescent Park Dining Hall. Sunday Bakes May 24, 27, 30 (Memorial Day), 31, June 7–14. Open daily for season June 21, 12 to 6:30 P.M. Special 5 o'clock bake every day." Lyon ran the bakes until the hurricane of 1938. (Ed Serowik Sr.)

The Crescent Park Shore Dining Hall is shown here shortly after the hurricane of 1938. The storm destroyed the pier and the southern part of the Comet roller coaster, but the dinner hall survived mostly intact. (Ed Serowik Sr.)

The park was purchased by a group of concessionaires, including Arthur R. Simmons and Frederick McCusker, in 1951. Here, Fred McCusker (with the tongs) moves blocks of pig iron in preparation for a clambake. Baskets of rockweed wait on the sidelines. The iron blocks were used instead of stones because they could be used over and over, and they radiated a uniform heat. The employee with the apron was named Sully; the other two are unidentified. (Ray Simmons.)

CRESCENT PARK SHORE DINNERS

No. 1
Park Special · · · · · · · · · · **$1.25**
TAX INCLUDED

Old Fashioned Rhode Island Clam Chowder
Crescent Park's Famous Clam Cakes
Sliced Cold Watermelon

No. 2
Regular Shore Dinner · · · · · · · · **$3.00**
TAX INCLUDED

Old Fashioned Rhode Island Clam Chowder
Crescent Park's Famous Clam Cakes
Steamed Clams with Drawn Butter
Fish Fried or Baked with French Fries
With Petukquineg Stuffing
Cole Slaw Salad
Sweet Corn in Season
White & Dark Bread - Creamery Butter
Sliced Cold Watermelon

No. 3
Lobster Shore Dinner · · · · · · · · **$4.00**
TAX INCLUDED

Old Fashioned Rhode Island Clam Chowder
Crescent Park's Famous Clam Cakes
Steamed Clams with Drawn Butter
Fish Fried or Baked with French Fries
With Petukquineg Stuffing
Cole Slaw Salad
Sweet Corn in Season
Whole Lobster
Rolls and Brown Bread — Creamery Butter
Sliced Cold Watermelon

4% RHODE ISLAND SALES TAX ON ALL ITEMS E

From the Sea

Crescent Park Famous
CLAM CHOWDER
50¢

Crescent Park Famous
CLAM CAKES
50¢

FRESH
STEAMED CLAMS
HOT DRAWN BUTTER
75¢

FRIED CLAMS
TO TAKE OUT
pint $1.20
½ pint 65¢

FISH and CHIPS
IN A BASKET
Tartar Sauce
65¢

FRIED SHRIMPS
IN A BASKET
95¢
Tartar Sauce
with French Fries

HOT or COLD
BOILED LOBSTER
Cole Slaw — French Fried Pot.
Drawn Butter
$2.25

LOBSTER ROLL
$1.00

A menu from the 1950s lists the delights awaiting patrons of both the Crescent Park Shore Dinner Hall and Crescent Park Inn. The majority of these items can still be found on the menus of Rhode Island clam shacks today—only the prices have changed! (Both, Ed Serowik Sr.)

CRESCENT PARK INN

Fresh Shrimp Cocktail .90   Tomato Juice .20
½ doz. Little Necks on the half shell .65
Clam Chowder, bowl .45

Seafarin' Dinners

Fried Clams, Tartar Sauce, French Fries and Cole Slaw 1.50
Lobster Salad Plate, Potato Salad, Cole Slaw, Boil Egg, Tom. 2.40
Baked Stuffed Haddock, Mashed Potatoes, Cole Slaw,
Dinner Roll 1.10
Fried Fillet Haddock, French Fried Potatoes, Cole Slaw, Roll 1.10

Landlubbers Fare

¼ Fried Chicken in a basket .85
½ Broiled Chicken, F.F. or Mashed Potato, Peas,
Cranberry Sauce 1.75
½ Fried Chicken with French Fries, Peas, Cranberry Sauce 1.75
Roast Stuffed Turkey Dinner, Mashed Potatoes, Peas,
Cranberry Sauce 1.60
Hot Turkey Sandwich, Mashed Potatoes, Peas,
Cranberry Sauce 1.10
French Fries .25
Corn on the Cob .20
Lettuce Tomato Salad .25

Sandwiches

Tuna Salad .45   Cheese .35   Cold Sliced Turkey .70
Egg Salad .40   Chicken Salad .50   Let. and Tomato .35

above served with Lettuce, Pickle, and Potato Chips
Frankfurters .25

Dessert

Pie .25   Ice Cream .25   Watermelon .25
Pie a la Mode .45   Bread Pudding .25   Jello .25

Beverages

Coffee with Cream .15   Tea .15   Milk .15
Soda .15   Iced Coffee .15
Coke, Orange, Ginger Ale

Beer
12 OZ. BOTTLE

Hanleys Pilsner .40   Budweiser .45
Narragansett Lager .40   Rupperts .45
Croft Ale .40   Schlitz .45

XCEPT SHORE DINNERS

This is a rare view of the Crescent Inn, which was part of the shore dining hall. Ray Simmons recalls that "it was actually a long beer bar. It was called the Knotty Pine Inn at one time and later the Ranch Room. People walked alongside this room in order to reach the entrance to the Shore Dinner Hall down by the pier. The building to the right of the Crescent Inn was called the Patio. Clam cakes and chowder were served here. This building was built after the original 200-seat Crescent Inn burned in a fire in 1953. Both the Shore Dinner Hall and the original Crescent Inn were served by the same giant kitchen." (East Providence Historical Society.)

This 1950s postcard, showcasing Crescent Park's "World Famous Shore Dinners," is the perfect card to inspire envy in the folks back home. A blurb on the back notes that the hall is air-conditioned, offers views of "beautiful Narragansett Bay," and is "the world's largest dinner hall in continuous operation." This last statement is true—Rocky Point was closed for almost a decade after the 1938 hurricane. (Louis McGowan.)

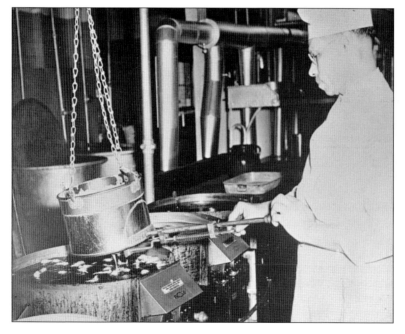

Crescent Park dining hall cook Manuel DeLumba is making clam cakes in this c. 1956 photograph. Ray Simmons, whose family owned the park from 1951 to 1967, recalls that "Manny had enormous hands and carefully measured the ingredients by the handsful." (Ed Serowik Sr.)

This is possibly the very clam cake dispenser used by Manuel DeLumba in the previous photograph. In operation, the lever on the handle is pulled back in a rapid repetitive motion, opening an aperture at the bottom of the container and allowing dollops of clam cake batter to fall into the hot oil. For places like Crescent Park that served a very high volume, this method was vastly superior to scooping by hand. (Ed Serowik Sr.)

Guests bought tickets for shore dinners, just as they did for rides, as shown by this Crescent Park shore dinner ticket from the 1960s. This ticket guaranteed one a smorgasbord of gastronomic delights—as much as a stomach could hold! (Ed Serowik Sr.)

Ray Simmons stated that these pictures, outside the Crescent Park Shore Dining Hall, were taken in the early 1960s. "They were taken on a normal Sunday. The hall could seat around 2,000 people at one time. In earlier days some company outings of 5,000 or more would require several seatings." (Both, Ray Simmons.)

In this early 1960s view of Crescent Park Shore Dining Hall, there is hardly an empty seat in the house. The large arched windows allowed natural light to flood the cavernous space even on overcast days. (Ed Serowick Sr..)

This candid photograph offers a glimpse inside the Crescent Park Shore Dining Hall kitchen in 1968. Big John, one of the head cooks (in the cap), works at one of the giant stainless steel chowder pots while two staff members look on. (Riondo Ribeiro.)

Crescent Park cook Rio Ribeiro seemingly levitates outside the shore dinner hall in 1969 as five coworkers look on. From left to right are Mike Giuliano, Karen Stroup, Emerson Torrey, Vin Giuliano, and Carl Ecklund. (Riondo Ribeiro.)

Shenanigans! The health inspector would surely have something to say about kitchen worker Neal Britto hiding inside a 40-gallon Crescent Park chowder kettle in 1970. (Riondo Ribeiro.)

Five Crescent Park Shore Dining Hall servers pause for a photograph in 1970. From left to right are Debbie Salaimen, unidentified, Gail DiGiannantonio, Denise Kuhn, and Laura Graff. Don't forget to tip! (Riondo Ribeiro.)

Park owners declared bankruptcy in 1975, and the park closed for good after the 1977 season. The Alhambra Ballroom was claimed by fire in 1969, and fires likewise destroyed the midway in March 1980 and the shore dining hall and Crescent Inn (shown here in full flame) in July 1984. Today, only the Looff Carousel, a National Historic Landmark, remains. (Charles Hall.)

The Stone Bridge Hotel in Tiverton was located opposite Grinnell's Beach and the old stone bridge that connected Portsmouth to the mainland. In the early 1900s, the hotel advertised it was "famous for its broiled live lobsters and R.I. broiler chickens" and noted it was the "Home of automobilists." (Louis McGowan.)

One of Stone Bridge Hotel's many dining rooms was on a "broad veranda overlook[ing] the beautiful Sakonnet River." In the 1940s and 1950s, the hotel boasted in advertisements that it was listed in *Gourmet's Guide to Good Eating.* Opened in the late 1890s, the building was taken down in the 1990s. (Portsmouth Free Library, John T. Pierce Sr. Collection.)

Philip W. Almy owned the dining hall at Sakonnet Point (shown here about 1907) in Little Compton, as well as the ferry that would take visitors there. A round-trip ticket on the ferry included a shore dinner. The hall, also known as the Clam House, was destroyed in the hurricane of 1938. The spot was later occupied by the Fo'c's'le. (CSM.)

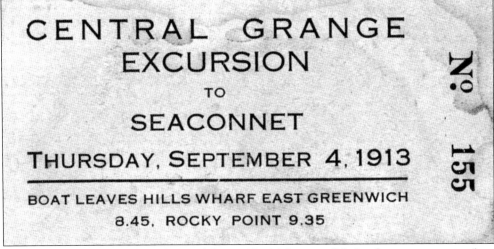

CENTRAL GRANGE
EXCURSION
TO
SEACONNET
THURSDAY, SEPTEMBER 4, 1913

No. 155

BOAT LEAVES HILLS WHARF EAST GREENWICH
8.45, ROCKY POINT 9.35

In 1913, a boat carried members of Central Grange No. 34, Patrons of Husbandry, on an excursion from East Greenwich to Sakonnet Point, with a stop at Rocky Point. (Warwick Historical Society.)

This aerial photograph shows Thomas Cashman's Amusement Park in Island Park, Portsmouth, in 1927. The large building at left center contained the shore dinner hall, dance hall, and penny arcade. The short-lived park opened in 1925–1926 and was so badly damaged by the 1938 hurricane that it never reopened. (Portsmouth Free Library, John T. Pierce Sr. Collection.)

The Tent on the Beach opened on Easton's Beach in Newport around 1880. An advertisement from the period touts "CLAM DINNERS" with "Clams and other fixings, cooked in the old-fashioned Narragansett Indian style, with Seaweed, Etc." Proprietor Walter Sherman and manager W. Henry Taylor also offered "Gents', Ladies' and Children's Bathing Costumes made to order in any style, at shortest notice." (CSM.)

In January 1918, *Providence Magazine* described the scene at Newport's Easton's Beach as one where swimming was of secondary importance. "Newport Beach presents surf bathing as an adjunct of its shore resort, specializing more in its clambakes, cafes and an interesting variety of attractions more or less vaudevillian, than on its bathing opportunities." This postcard view is of the interior of the Lunch Pavilion at Easton's Beach. (DNS.)

The figures sweeping outside the open-air Hygeia Café at Easton's Beach in Newport promise that the establishment lived up to its name (Hygieia was the Greek goddess of cleanliness). The Hygeia Café was owned and operated by African American brothers J.T. Allen and D.B. Allen. J.T. Allen was born in North Carolina on November 22, 1867. In 1893, J.T. and his brother D.B. arrived in Newport and soon established the Hygeia Café and the dining room in the basement of the Perry Mansion on Touro Street. The Hygeia Café pavilion at Easton's Beach burned to the ground on September 22, 1897. In this photograph, an awning advertises Hassard's Whipped Cream Soda, a unique offering that surely drove sales at the soda fountain. (PPL.)

A stroll down the boardwalk at Easton's Beach in Newport offered numerous diversions, including (as shown here) a shore dinner restaurant. Seen in the distance is the Scenic Railway, the beach's first roller coaster. (PPL.)

Block Island was no slouch in the shore dinner department. Day-trippers might hop off the ferry and stride into an establishment such as the one at left on Front Street, while those well-to-do enough to spend a night or a week in one of the island's many elegant hotels could have their desires fulfilled in a sumptuous dining room. This postcard view is from 1905. (Louis McGowan.)

Run by the Mott family, who were farmers since their arrival in the 1700s, the Narragansett Inn (1912) was the last great hotel built on the island. It originally was a shore dinner hall, and the inn grew up around it. The original dinner hall is now used as the inn's dining room. (CSM.)

Narragansett Pier at the turn of the 20th century rivaled Newport as a playground for the wealthy. The original pier casino burned to the ground in a magnificent conflagration in 1900 and was replaced with this one, referred to as Sherry's New Casino, about 1905. (Louis McGowan.)

Before the original casino was constructed at Narragansett Pier between 1883 and 1886, the pier was known for "broiled live lobsters." As no one knows who thought of it first, two men, restaurateur William H. Billington and saloonkeeper Edward Simonds, are credited equally with developing this innovation in the late 1860s. Legend has it that the casino at Narragansett Pier was also the birthplace of Clams Casino. (Louis McGowan.)

The Buttonwoods was founded in Warwick in 1871 by the Reverend Moses Bixby of Providence's Cranston Street Baptist Church as a place for members of his congregation to spend their summers. The *Providence Journal*, in 1930, noted that at a hotel there run by a Colonel Lyman, "the guests have been much pleased with the broiled live lobsters which he sets forth every Sunday evening." This engraving dates to around 1886. (CSM.)

The Rhode Island clambake, and later the shore dinner, was the source of the fame and glory of Rocky Point. It was for the taste of clams that crowds thronged to its "rocky" shores. William Winslow first built a shore dinner hall there in 1859. His wife, Phebe, prepared the clambake. By the 1870s, that first shore dinner hall, with a fountain in the middle, had grown considerably larger. (New York Public Library.)

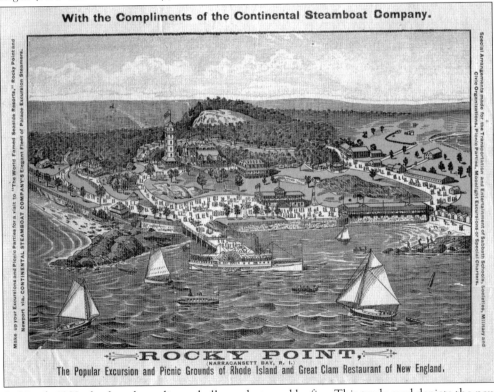

In March 1883, the first shore dinner hall was destroyed by fire. This trade card depicts the new Queen Anne dining hall, the second shore dinner hall. The reverse of the card boasts that "the services of 'Jerry' the famous Indian Chowder and fish cook, have been secured, who for nearly half a century has served the people on the shore of Rocky Point, and it may now be truly said that Rocky Point furnishes the public the original and old fashioned Rhode Island clam bake established by our fathers." (Warwick Historical Society.)

Here is a rare view of the interior of the shore dinner hall from around 1882. Patrons sat on tall stools at a long communal table. The waiter in the foreground appears to be offering a plate of steamers. Note the shelf running the length of the table for gentlemen's hats. (PPL.)

This postcard of the second shore dinner hall shows that it rested on pilings that placed diners out in the bay along with watercraft. By the early 1880s, it was estimated that Rocky Point had already hosted over 2.4 million visitors, with 260,000 bushels of clams having been used in that time in its bakes and in making chowders and clam cakes. (DNS.)

This note in Randall Harrington's hand is perhaps confirming a shore dinner outing. Harrington first leased Rocky Point from the Continental Steamboat Company in 1888, then bought it outright in 1910. Harrington died in 1918, but his wife and son held onto the property until 1945, relying on others to operate the park. (Warwick Historical Society.)

C. E. LYON
The man who made the Rhode
Island Clambake famous.

NARRAGANSETT Bay and its surrounding shores are the background of many historical events coincident with the early settlement of Rhode Island. To the aboriginal indian, who in great numbers were the original possessors, we are indebted for the custom from which has grown a State and National institution known as the Rhode Island Clambake. Huge mounds of shells have been discovered near the spot we now occupy, from which were taken stone implements of war and husbandry, that are mute evidences of the antiquity and origin of this repast.

With the passing centuries, generation after generation have made pilgrimages here to refresh the "inner man," and to perpetuate the ancient custom. We know not who in the forgotten past may have drawn from land and sea and made the feast, but for a score and seven years one man has led all others in the art, and we today are the judges of his skill.

Charles E. Lyon, the man who made the Rhode Island clambake famous, is one of the great names of clam cookery and came to Rocky Point around 1900. He was also associated with Field's Point and Crescent Point and may be the person responsible for the tradition that Rocky Point's chowder contained tomato puree. This portrait of Lyon was printed in a pamphlet from the American Optical Manufacturer's Association clambake on July 21, 1916, which includes an intriguing story about the origin of clambakes. (Warwick Historical Society.)

As shown in this c. 1907 postcard, the clambake portion of the shore dinner at Rocky Point was prepared in a space behind the shore dinner hall. The sheer volume of clams is impressive, especially when considering this is only one day's worth. (Louis McGowan.)

This is another view of the second Rocky Point shore dinner hall, this time from the back, or landward side. Note the open sides allowing for the free flow of air on hot summer days. The clambake area is to the right, behind the picket fence. (Louis McGowan.)

A second floor was added over the second shore dinner hall around 1925, when an advertisement promised a bigger, brighter, better dining hall, with no more waiting in line. During the hurricane of 1938, the second floor fell through the first. (DNS.)

The third shore dinner hall, depicted on this letterhead, opened in 1949 after three abandoned attempts to rebuild it in the previous decade. John Gomes, who had been the chef prior to 1938, was brought back to oversee the kitchen. As a sign of confidence, the new dinner hall was extended 30 feet further into the bay. Fortunately, the new owners bought insurance on the building because, in 1954, during Hurricane Carol, Conrad Ferla watched the roof of his shore dinner hall fly off and into the parking lot. (Warwick Historical Society.)

The fourth and final shore dinner hall was constructed very quickly, opening in 1955. It was built of cement blocks and steel, set away from the water on a ledge and 20 feet higher than the previous buildings to protect it from tidal surges. Designed by Lewis Zampini, the building was 300 feet long and 100 feet wide, with take-out windows along the water-side street level for clam cakes and chowder "to go." (PPL.)

This postcard offers a glimpse into the interior of the last of the great shore dinner halls. People ordering all-you-can-eat clam cakes and chowder were not allowed to sit with those who ordered shore dinners, sometimes causing families to have to split up (for lunch or dinner anyway). When the wait staff decided diners had eaten enough of the all-you-can-eat fare, they dropped a giant roll of paper onto the end of the table as a hint that it was time to make way for the next seating. (Warwick Historical Society.)

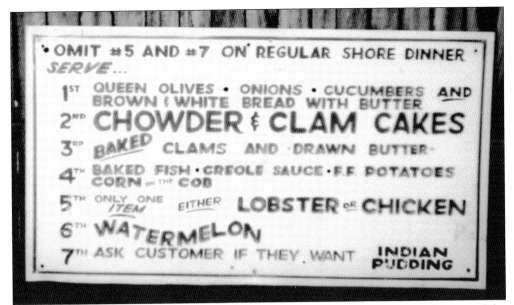

This sign instructing the wait staff on the order in which to serve the various elements of the shore dinner dates from around the 1960s and probably hung in the kitchen area. Indian pudding is a porridge made of cornmeal, milk, and molasses. (Warwick Historical Society.)

Rocky Point Amusement Park closed for good in 1996, and by February 2001, the date of this photograph, the famous shore dinner hall was already showing signs of neglect. It was demolished in July 2014, having been further degraded by vandals and the elements. (CSM.)

Ephraim Thurber held the first public clambake at Field's Point in Providence in 1849. Russell Fenner followed, adding clam cakes, sweet potatoes, baked bluefish, sliced onions and cucumbers, watermelon, and Indian pudding to the menu. Field's Point reached its acme under Col. S.S. Atwell, who ran it from about 1887 to 1910. (Louis McGowan.)

Field's Point, named for Thomas Field, whose 37-acre farm occupied the point, was, in the late 1880s, a bucolic setting. The City of Providence ran a smallpox hospital there and leased part of the land to the clambake facility. The point offered the nearest clambakes to the city, and workers could easily visit it for their midday meals. The facility boasted of serving fresh bakes every day at 12:30, 2:30, and 5:00. (PPL.)

Field's Point had both an exposed sandy beach and a hidden spot for bathers called Old Maid's Cove. The point was so popular under Colonel Atwell, especially on Sundays, when many other businesses were closed, that he had to enlarge the dining room until there was no more room to do so. (DNS.)

Many of the well-known names of the clambake trade got their start at Field's Point, among them Charles Lyon of Rocky Point and Thomas Crowell of Crescent Park. Crowell, who started at Field's Point at age 11, once divulged that one of his trade secrets for clambakes was to scorch the rockweed before sealing it in the bake. (DNS.)

Clambakes at Field's Point came to an end in 1910 with the retirement of Colonel Atwell. The first of many changes to the point began at that time, and the area assumed a much more industrial character. Atwell auctioned the clam sheds, buildings, boilers, and kettles in 1911. Colonel Harrington of Rocky Point and Crescent Park was an enthusiastic bidder on the equipment, which netted $1,100. (PPL.)

In this c. 1910s postcard, Eitner's Hotel Lincoln in Staten Island, New York, advertises "Rhode Island Shore Dinner" in its windows. While New York is only a couple of states away, this is an example of Rhode Island's famous feast flourishing far from home. (New York Public Library.)

Three

AUNT CARRIE'S

Dining together on April 17, 1951, are, from left to right, Gov. John G. Roberts, Carrie Cooper (Aunt Carrie), and her husband, Ulysses Grant Cooper (Uncle Lys). In 1938, Ulysses was elected on the Republican ticket to the General Assembly and held that office until his death in 1953. Each year, he hosted all the members of the House at a clambake at Aunt Carrie's, and on those days, there were no Republicans or Democrats, just friends of Uncle Lys and Aunt Carrie. (Aunt Carrie's.)

Aunt Carrie's, shown here in its earliest incarnation, is the oldest family-operated, continuously run clam shack. Carrie Campbell (1875–1964) was born in the mill village of Lafayette, near North Kingstown, Rhode Island. She moved to Connecticut to marry Ulysses Cooper, and the pair eventually summered in Point Judith. Known as Uncle Lys, Ulysses Cooper (1870–1953) was born in Norwich, Connecticut. He attended Mount Herman Bible School in New Hampshire and was a lay preacher at one time. He and Carrie originally opened a small establishment near the lighthouse serving lemonade and clam fritters, but in 1925 purchased the current location. As early as the 1930s, Aunt Carrie's clam cakes were being called everything from "the choicest tidbits from the great Atlantic's benevolent cupboard" to "internationally famous." Her clam cakes were so good that it is no wonder that many thought she had invented them. The Coopers' 16-year-old daughter Gertrude poses in front of the lemonade stand. She later operated the restaurant and was often mistaken for Aunt Carrie herself. (Aunt Carrie's.)

At one time, shore dinners were cooked and served on the beach, which was also a campground. Erosion has claimed much of the land that once served as the campground. (Aunt Carrie's.)

Prior to the hurricane of 1938, many families enjoyed a vacation at the Coopers' campground. It was billed as the largest parking and camping ground in the east, with 1,000 feet of frontage on the Atlantic Ocean. (Aunt Carrie's.)

Bathers cavort at Aunt Carrie's beach. Many credit Aunt Carrie's with bringing development to the Point Judith area. Today, some of the most popular beaches in Rhode Island are nearby. (Aunt Carrie's.)

The card reads: "Aunt Carrie's Tourist Camp, shore and lobster dinners a specialty, Point Judith, R.I." Ulysses and Carrie Cooper stand with their daughter Virginia in the 1920s. The Socony station eventually moved across the street. (Louis McGowan.)

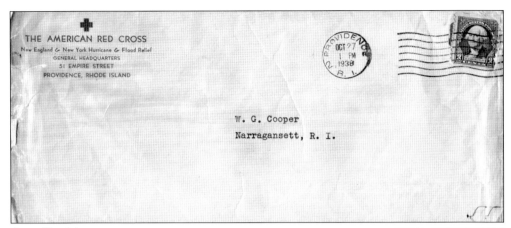

W. G. Cooper
Narragansett, R. I.

Aunt Carrie's was not immune from world events. This correspondence from the Red Cross is a memento of a lifesaving operation after the hurricane of 1938. During World War II, the campground was a military base, and several military officers lived upstairs at Aunt Carrie's. Ulysses was (ironically) chairman of the rationing board and served as one of the watchers in the Air Observation Corps. Tragically, Carrie and Ulysses's only son, Stuart, was declared missing in action on February 14, 1948, after the bomber he was piloting was shot down off Bougainville in the Pacific. (Aunt Carrie's.)

A bill for two bushels of steamer clams dated 1939 demonstrates that Aunt Carrie's was back in business after the great hurricane the year before. One of the few changes to Aunt Carrie's clam cake recipe over the years has been the addition of more clams, to satisfy customers' expectations. (Aunt Carrie's.)

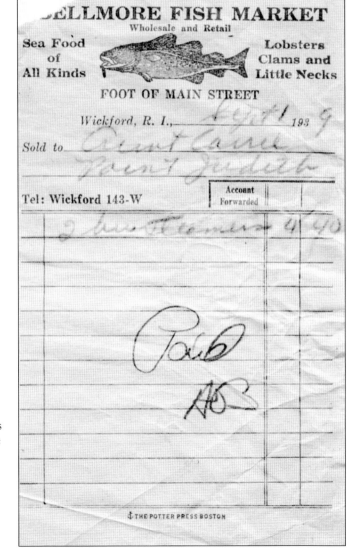

BELLMORE FISH MARKET
Wholesale and Retail

Sea Food of All Kinds

Lobsters Clams and Little Necks

FOOT OF MAIN STREET

Wickford, R. I., _____ 193

Sold to _____

Tel: Wickford 143-W

Account Forwarded

‡ THE POTTER PRESS BOSTON

Uncle Lys and Aunt Carrie watch as some good-natured horseplay goes on—exposing a woman's tan line. Uncle Lys's favorite saying was "come aboard and bring your dory," used for many years in Aunt Carrie's advertisements. (Aunt Carrie's.)

Aunt Carrie and Uncle Lys also served shore dinners at the Kingston Fair Grounds, Brooklyn Fair, and the Stratford Springs Fair. Here, Uncle Lys hosts a clambake for employees, possibly at the Kingston Fair. Second-generation owners Gertrude and William Foy thanked employees with a party after Labor Day at which they cooked and served a full turkey. Afterwards, they did the cleaning up themselves. (Aunt Carrie's.)

The tricycle in this 1956 postcard (behind the Volkswagen) belonged to Elsie Foy's husband, William, the third-generation owner of Aunt Carrie's, reminding the viewer that the restaurant was very much a part of family life. Family Thanksgiving dinners were held in the restaurant with the tables pushed together. (Aunt Carrie's.)

A menu in the handwriting of second-generation owner Gertrude Foy shows that the bill of fare has not changed much in the last century. The interior is similarly unaltered, including the green and yellow color scheme. (Aunt Carrie's.)

COMPLETE DINNERS

ALL DINNERS FOR ONE PERSON ONLY
No Substitutions

Rhode Island Shore Dinner		$1.90
Without Lobster		
Rhode Island Shore Dinner		3.15
With Whole Cold Boiled Lobster		
Rhode Island Shore Dinner		3.90
With Live Broiled Lobster		

INCLUDED WITH THE SHORE DINNERS
All of the Chowder, Clam Cakes and Steamed Clams That You Can Eat
Fish and Vegetables   Brown Bread and Butter
Choice of: Watermelon, Ice Cream or Indian Pudding

	Dinner	Plate Only
Fried Scallops	1.40	1.10
Fried Shrimp	1.40	1.10
Fried Clams	1.40	1.10
Seafood Platter	1.65	1.35
(Fried Clams, Shrimp, Fish and Scallops)		
Broiled Flounder	1.40	1.10
Broiled Mackerel	1.40	1.10
Broiled Swordfish	1.55	1.25
Cold or Hot Boiled Lobster	2.00	1.70
Live Broiled Lobster	2.75	2.45
Allow 30 Min. for Preparation		
Lobster Salad	2.50	2.20
Broiled Pork Chops	1.60	1.30
Broiled Lamb Chops	2.00	1.70
Broiled Steak	2.50	2.20
We Are Not Responsible For Any Steak Ordered Well Done		
Broiled Chicken	2.00	1.70
Chicken Salad	1.75	1.45

INCLUDED WITH THE ABOVE DINNERS;
Cup of Chowder, French Fries, Vegetable, Bread and Butter,
Coffee and Dessert

Steamed Clam Dinner		1.20

INCLUDED WITH THE STEAMED CLAMS:
Cup of Chowder, Bread and Butter, Melted Butter, Clam Broth,
Coffee and Dessert

CHILDREN'S DINNERS
FOR CHILDREN ONLY

Lobster Salad	1.40
Swordfish	.85
Broiled Flounder	.75
Broiled Mackerel	.75
Fried Clams	.75
Hamburg	.75
Fried Scallops	.75
Lamb Chop	1.25
Pork Chop	1.05

INCLUDED WITH THE DINNERS
Cup of Chowder, Potato, Vegetable, Bread and Butter
Milk, Small Ice Cream or Watermelon

Current owner Elsie Foy recalls changing clam fritters to clam cakes on the menu, defying the notion that fritters is a term foreign to Rhode Island. Interestingly, this particular menu uses both names. When Elsie Foy started, the restaurant served two kinds of chowder, tomato and plain. Milk chowder was a relatively recent addition. (Both, Aunt Carrie's.)

A LA CARTE MENU

Juices *(Tomato, Orange, Grapefruit, Pineapple)*		.15
Clam Chowder		
Bowl		.30
Cup		.20
Cup of Clam Broth		.15
Shrimp Cocktail		.50
Lobster Cocktail		.95
Clam Fritters		.60 per doz.
Order of Fried Clams		.60
Order of Fried Shrimp or Scallops		.70
Pan of Steamed Clams *Clam Broth and Melted Butter*		.75
Pan of Clams, Boiled Lobster and Melted Butter		2.00
Lobster Saute—French Fries, Salad		1.50
With Dressing, Potato and Vegetable		
Half A Roast Chicken		1.50
Large Hamburg Plate		.85
Child's Hamburg Plate		.50
Lobster Meat & Mayonnaise on Lettuce		1.75
Cold Boiled Lobster with Melted Butter		1.25
Live Broiled Lobster, Melted Butter		2.00
Fish & Chips	Small .45	Large .75
French Fries	Small .15	Large .25
Toast		.10
Peas & Boiled Potato		.25
Vegetable Plate	Small .30	Large .55

SANDWICHES

Fried Clam or Shrimp Roll	.35	Tuna	.40
		Steak	.60
Lobster Sandwich or Roll	.85	Frankfort	.20
		Hamburg	.25
Sliced Chicken	.55	Cheeseburger	.35
Chicken Salad	.50	Sliced Cheese	.20
Bacon, Lettuce & Tomato	.45	Lettuce & Tomato	.20
		Bacon	.25

DRINKS

Tea, Coffee, Milk		.10
Iced Tea or Coffee *10c Extra With Dinners*		.20
Milk Shakes		.20
Cabinets		.30

DESSERTS

Ice Cream	.15
Home Made Pies	.20
Indian Pudding with Ice Cream	.20
Watermelon	.15

This genial looking fellow is William Foy, who with his wife, Gertrude, was the second generation of the family to run Aunt Carrie's. Bill summered at the campground and eventually worked at the restaurant, which is where he met his wife. "Come aboard and meet your dory" could be an alternate motto for Aunt Carrie's seasonal workers, many of whom met their spouses there. (Aunt Carrie's.)

This sign was created in the 1970s or 1980s by an unidentified Aunt Carrie's employee who considered herself or himself a member of the "Chowder Chuckers of America, Local 7420," with the motto, "A clam cake in every hand, some chowder in every pot." The faded letters in the center incongruously spell out, "Down with cave men." (Aunt Carrie's.)

Aunt Carrie did not invent the clam cake, but she certainly perfected it. Shaped with antique spoons and fried in lard, no two Aunt Carrie's clam cakes are ever alike in appearance. It is a general rule of thumb that the farther south one goes in Rhode Island, the bigger the clam cakes. Aunt Carrie's is about as south as one can get. (CSM.)

Aunt Carrie, left, and staff assemble for a group portrait in the 1920s. In 2007, Aunt Carrie's won the James Beard Foundation's America's Classics Award. The restaurant will celebrate its 100th anniversary in 2020. (Aunt Carrie's.)

Four

CLAM SHACKS

Champlin's Seafood Deck (then just called Champlin's Market) began as a simple wholesale and retail fish market in the 1920s. In 1937, owner Harry Champlin (pictured here in 1932) began selling a clear chowder to the retail crowd, starting the business's evolution into a full-fledged clam shack. (Champlin's Seafood Deck.)

Hurricane Carol slammed into New York and southern New England on August 31, 1954, shortly after high tide. The resulting 10- to 15-foot storm surge destroyed everything in its path along the coast, while inland, sustained winds as high as 90 miles per hour wrecked homes and businesses and uprooted trees. Champlin's Market fared a little better than some—it still had a few walls standing. (Champlin's Seafood Deck.)

It was not until 1970 that Champlin's became a full-fledged restaurant. That same year, by popular demand, red and white clam chowder were added to the menu. In 2007, Champlin's vice president T. Brian Handrigan estimated that clear still made up 50 percent of chowder sales, with red and white garnering only 30 percent and 20 percent, respectively. (Champlin's Seafood Deck.)

By the 1980s, a second floor was added to contain the restaurant, allowing that part of the business some measure of security against tidal surges. Downstairs, the seafood market continues operation in its original space. All day, every day, fishing boats tie up at the docks behind the building and unload their catches of flounder, haddock, shrimp, salmon, scup, tuna, bass, mackerel, butterfish, codfish, scrod, squid, herring, swordfish, lobster, clams, oysters, and quahogs. (Champlin's Seafood Deck.)

In 1990, Jimmy Champlin sold the restaurant and seafood market to a partnership, including local entrepreneurs Stephen Heard and T. Brian Handrigan (1937–2015). Within 10 years, the restaurant expanded from seating 60 customers to seating around 300. For a time, a satellite market, Champlin's of Wickford, operated in North Kingstown. (Champlin's Seafood Deck.)

George's of Galilee began as George's Lunch, a tiny place named for its owner, possibly George Partelow (sources are unclear). Around 1948, it was purchased by a bakery truck driver and his wife, Norman and Edna Durfee, who soon built up an early-morning clientele of Galilean fishermen. George's Lunch is shown here in 1933. (Kevin Durfee.)

Breakfast became so integral to the business's bottom line that "Lunch" was soon dropped from the name. Here is Norman Durfee behind the counter around 1950. (Kevin Durfee.)

"The fish you eat today with me slept last night in the deep blue sea," boasts the back of this postcard. A typical fried seafood platter served at George's in the 1950s consisted of a plate filled with fried fish, clams and scallops, a clam cake, lobster salad and coleslaw, with sides of salad, French fries, clam chowder, and dinner rolls. The tablecloth patterned with lobsters and clams is an especially fine touch. (DNS.)

Shown here in the mid-1960s, George's, under Norman Durfee, was still a somewhat modest business. In 1969, prompted by health issues, Durfee passed the restaurant on to his three sons, Don, Wayne, and Richard, who expanded the building and the menu. (Louis McGowan.)

George's Channel Lounge (shown here around 1965) offered stunning views of the Galilee channel, through which the Block Island ferries passed within clam cake throwing distance of patrons on the deck. George's of Galilee is today the largest waterfront restaurant in the state, seating over 500 patrons in six dining rooms on two levels. (DNS.)

Jimmy's Port Side Restaurant in Galilee is a third-generation family business, run by Jim Petrella Jr. and his mother, Deb, and originally opened by Jim's grandfather in 1956. The eponymous "Jimmy" was Jim Petrella Sr., who took over the restaurant from his father and ran it with his wife until his death in 2007. Jimmy's Port Side Restaurant location, directly across from the Block Island Ferry, makes it an easy choice for clam cakes and chowder, either coming or going. (CSM.)

"TUNA CAPITAL OF THE WORLD"
GALILEE, R. I.

The Fo'c's'le, shown here in the early 1960s, was located in Galilee about where Buster Krab's Beach Bar and Burger Shack is now. In 1983, they boasted of their view "overlooking beautiful Galilee Harbor and Breachway." The term "Fo'c's'le" or Forecastle refers to the forward section of a ship containing the sailors' living quarters. All those apostrophes confused author David Stone as a young child, but he loved their tuna salad rolls. (CSM.)

Skip's Dock—named for original owner Ernest "Skip" Streeter (1878–1954)—has been a seafood market and bait shop since about 1906. At that time, Jerusalem was just a tiny fishing village, the Point Judith Pond Breachway had not yet been opened, and Potter's Pond was the main port. The original breachway was west of Matunuck Beach. This artistically enhanced photograph dates from 1937. (Bob and Ingrid Trager.)

Here is Skip Streeter feeding the seagulls (a handwritten note on the back says "Dad and his 'pets'") in October 1951. An energetic fellow, Streeter was burdened with a bad stutter, which he combated by speaking slowly and deliberately. (Bob and Ingrid Trager.)

Unidentified employees shuck scallops inside Skip's Dock in this undated postcard. Skip's was both a wholesale and retail business, and he bought most of his product—shellfish, lobsters, and swordfish—direct from fishermen who tied up at his dock. (Bob and Ingrid Trager.)

Skip's was owned by Jim and Muriel Hartley between 1951 and 1961 and was known as Jim's Dock (not to be confused with the clam shack of the same name opened up the street by Jim DeCubellis around 1971). The swordfish on the pole is a holdover from Skip Streeter's time. (Bob and Ingrid Trager.)

From 1961 to 1976, Skip's was owned by Ed and Jackie Baransky, who then sold it to Bob and Ingrid Trager, who still own it today. In addition to continuing business as a seafood market, the Tragers sold souvenirs and penny candy, and for a time, they rented boats. In 2013, they began selling prepared foods, like clam cakes, chowder, steamers, and lobster rolls. This postcard view dates from around 1986. (Louis McGowan.)

Disaster is an inevitability this close to the ocean. Skip's Dock witnessed the hurricane of 1938, Hurricanes Carol and Edna in 1954, the blizzard of 1978 (when the dock was damaged by tide-driven ice), the World Prodigy oil spill in 1989 (which severely affected the local lobster industry), and this July 1997 fire. Even an extraordinarily high tide can flood the building. In October 2012, Hurricane Sandy destroyed the whole dock, but Bob Trager and his sons managed to rebuild it in time to reopen the following June. (Bob and Ingrid Trager.)

Edward Duhamel was an East Providence chauffeur who began buying land in Charlestown. He eventually opened the Willows, a seasonal restaurant. Patrons continually lined up at the kitchen door of the Willows for Harriet Barnes Duhamel's clam fritters, so in 1950, Edward Duhamel decided to open a little shack with two deep fryers, a grill, and a gas stove to cook chowder. He called it the Car Hop. (Tammy Duhamel McLellan of the Hitching Post.)

The clam shack closed briefly when Jerry Duhamel Sr. left to serve in the Korean War. Jerry reopened the business in 1954 and named it the Hitching Post, a suggestion from his mother because he and his brother liked to hitch their horses to a post there and feed them ice cream cones. Here is Duhamel dressed as a woman as a gag with his best friend in October 1955. (Tammy Duhamel McLellan of the Hitching Post.)

This c. 1966 photograph shows the original Hitching Post behind the new building. Tammy Duhamel and brother Jerry Jr. play in the snow in the foreground. Tammy has been involved in the business since she was a child and remembers standing on Coca-Cola cases to take an order. (Tammy Duhamel McLellan of the Hitching Post.)

An employee at the old pass-through window pauses for refreshment in August 1973. Bucking tradition in the rest of Rhode Island, the Hitching Post has consistently called their clam cakes "fritters" since the days of the Willows. Their chowder dinner has always consisted of five fritters served with a bowl of clear chowder. (Tammy Duhamel McLellan of the Hitching Post.)

Guest chef Thelma tends to the bubbling fritters in the summer of 1993. Her husband was a regular cook at the Hitching Post. (Tammy Duhamel McLellan of the Hitching Post.)

Jerry Duhamel Sr. is shown here in the kitchen in 1993. Where there are quahogs and flour, there will soon be fritters. Duhamel passed away in 2013. His daughter Tammy, who is a teacher, carries on the tradition today. When asked why, she responded, "For dad." (Tammy Duhamel McLellan of the Hitching Post.)

WYOMING, RHODE ISLAND

Oysters were the McDonald's hamburgers of their day—cheap, fast, and ubiquitous. That they could be had even in little, out-of-the-way places like the village of Wyoming in Richmond is attested by this c. 1900 postcard. It is easy to imagine that these men have just finished a serious game of dirt-lot baseball and are ready for oysters and beer. (Tim Cranston and Rachel Peirce.)

Located at the corner of West Main Street and Post Road in Wickford, Emery's Clam Cake Shack operated from 1936 to 1960 under the ownership of Waldo and Carmen Emery. Wickford historian Tim Cranston recalls "clam cakes as big as baseballs" and blueberry pies made fresh each day in the house above the shack. Rhode Islanders of a certain age fondly recall stopping at Emery's on the way home from the beach. The shack was just recently torn down. (Tim Cranston and Rachel Peirce.)

This postcard depicts the Wickford Marina House. It was described as "a superb and beautiful waterfront restaurant overlooking historic Wickford Harbor and America's finest yacht basin." Locals do not seem to remember it, probably because it has changed so much over the years, including a second-story addition that for a time contained the Top of the Dock Lounge decorated with Paul Loring caricatures. (DNS.)

Gus's Restaurant at Oakland Beach in Warwick was established in 1924 by Gus and Frieda Gionis. The restaurant was popular for its famous hamburgers (made with onions and peppers), as well as clam cakes, Rhode Island clam chowder, and jumbo "cabinets" (the name for milkshakes in Rhode Island). The figure shown in the doorway here around 1935 may be Gus himself. (James Rengigas.)

Shown here around 1939 are Teddy Rengigas (at right) and three unidentified young ladies. Ipswich clams, harvested from the mudflats in and around Ipswich, Massachusetts, were (and are) famed for their tenderness and flavor. They are great steamed or fried. The lack of buildings in the background helps date the photograph to just after the hurricane of 1938. (James Rengigas.)

Siblings John Rengigas, Frieda Rengigas Gionis, and George Rengigas stand before the menu board of Gus's in the late 1970s. All the hand-printed additions are a sign of a cook who listens to what his customers want and is not afraid to try new things. (James Rengigas.)

Gus's Restaurant is on the right in this early 1980s photograph. Down the street is Mrs. Gus's Doughboys, an annex that was added around 1940. That stand was sold to Gaetano and Sally Gravino in 1989 and became Iggy's Doughboys and Chowder House. (James Rengigas.)

Frieda Gionis, the Mrs. Gus of Mrs. Gus's Doughboys, is caught in a free moment inside her shack. A doughboy is fried dough, sometimes garnished with powdered sugar or cinnamon sugar. The particular recipe served by Mrs. Gus was Greek in origin. (James Rengigas.)

This early 1980s photograph shows the former summer home of Rhode Island governor D. Russell Brown, built in 1908 at Oakland Beach in Warwick. In the 1940s, it was owned by Joseph L. Carrolo, who turned Oakland Beach into a tourist attraction. The house was sold out of the family in 1981 and opened as the Island View Inn. In 1986, it became Cherrystones, and in 2008, Top of the Bay. (Warwick Historical Society.)

Rocky Point Chowder House (shown here around 1990) was an effort to bring the Rocky Point shore dinner hall experience outside the park. There was this location in Oakland Beach (just up the street from Iggy's), one at the Rhode Island Mall, and another on Post Road, north of the airport. The Post Road location closed in 2008; the Oakland Beach location is now Iggy's Boardwalk Lobster and Clam Bar. (Warwick Historical Society.)

Seafood fans have already discovered Iggy's Doughboys and Chowder House in this c. 1990 photograph. Iggy's opened in 1989 on the site of Mrs. Gus's Doughboys in Oakland Beach. In the decades since, Iggy's has grown substantially, with renovations and expansions and a second location in Narragansett. (Warwick Historical Society.)

The Crow's Nest in Apponaug was originally opened as a clam shack in 1966 by Tom Kelly and Frank White of the Ponaug Marina. The business was sold several times over the years, but the restaurant always kept the name Crow's Nest. The picnic tables outside offered exciting views of both the cove and train tracks overhead. This photograph is from the early 1970s, when the building still clearly retained its clam shack nature. (Laurie Grann.)

By 1982, the Crow's Nest building had been expanded to become a full-fledged restaurant while still serving clam cakes and chowder. Sometime in the 1980s, the building was destroyed in a fire. It was rebuilt and then purchased by the current owners, John and Laurie Grann, in 1992. The restaurant remains open almost year-round, bringing a bit of summer into the colder months. (Laurie Grann.)

Sometimes even the allure of clam cakes and ice cream is not enough to ensure success. This little diner, run by Bob Larivee on his property on Plainfield Pike, just west of Peck Hill Road in Johnston, lasted only the summer of 1958. (Bob Larivee/Johnston Historical Society.)

Pictured is Downyflake, at the corner of Eddy and Weybosset Streets in Providence, around 1945 (now the site of a 7-Eleven). Downyflake was one of the first business franchises in the United States, dating back to the 1930s. Proudly displayed on the marquee are Autocrat Coffee and Saltesea Clam Chowder and Oysters, both Rhode Island companies. Autocrat is still in business; Saltesea, a subsidiary of American Oyster Company of Providence, was producing clear Rhode Island–style and creamy New England–style chowders as late as 1953. One of American Oyster Company's buildings, located on the Seekonk River at Fox Point, was purchased by Brown University in 1966 and now serves as headquarters for Brown's crew teams. (PPL.)

This postcard for Johnson's Hummocks Grille at 245 Allen's Avenue in Providence is much more spectacular in color. At top is the Daily Double: two baked stuffed lobsters, onion rings, French fries, clam cakes, and fried clams. At bottom is the Miniature Clambake: a split lobster, steamers, clam cakes, and fries. (Warwick Historical Society.)

Johnson's Hummocks Grille not only had a "Lobster Room," but also a "Neptune Room," a "State Room," a "Commodore Room," banquet rooms on the second floor, and (oddly for a seafood palace) a "Prime Rib Room." Once Route 95 was built, the restaurant could be easily spotted due to its large sign facing the highway. (Louis McGowan.)

LOOKING FOR LOBSTERS?... HERE THEY ARE!

. . . Fresh from Johnson's own salt water purifying tanks at Wickford, R. I., into the famous "LOBSTER ROOM". Any one of Johnson's four dining rooms will make a hit with you. Drop in on your next trip through Providence!

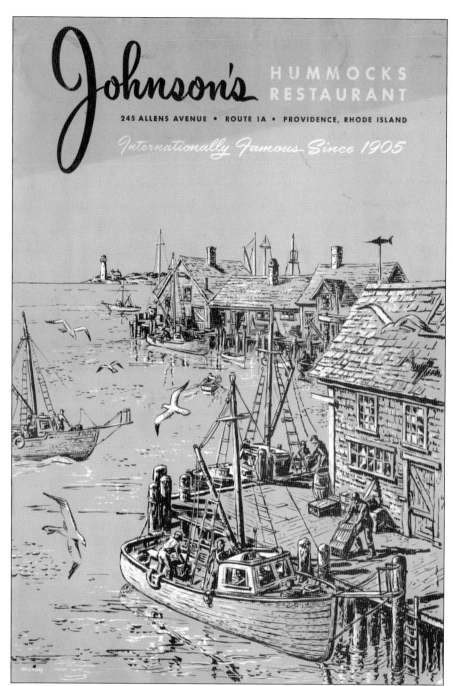

Johnson's Hummock's never forgot its Wickford roots and was proud of its lobster plant 17 miles from Providence in Wickford Harbor, near where the Johnson family got their start. Waitresses wore a lobster pin as part of their uniform. For many adults today, their main childhood memory of Johnson's Hummocks is that, after cleaning their plates, they could pick out a small toy from the large treasure chest at the front. The restaurant closed its doors for good on May 19, 1970. This menu probably dates from the late 1960s, when a cup of chowder was 30¢ and a broiled live 1.25-pound lobster was $3.75. (CSM.)

Located on Bristol Harbor, the Lobster Pot has been serving seafood since 1929 and is representative of the Rhode Island chowder house—a casual seafood restaurant offering much of the fare available at clam shacks but open year-round and with a bit more variety. This postcard from the 1940s boasts that the Lobster Pot is listed in Duncan Hines's *Adventures in Good Eating*, an early guide for explorers of local cuisine. (DNS.)

The Lobster Pot was completely destroyed in the 1938 hurricane, leaving nothing but bare ground. The rebuilt Lobster Pot's decor of nautical bric-a-brac, brass, and mounted fish is classic chowder house style. Its location on the East Bay is superbly suited for sunset views through its large windows. This view probably dates from the 1960s. (DNS.)

Flo's Clam Shack in Island Park, Portsmouth, was started around 1936 by two Tiverton sisters, Flora and Alice Helger. The first shack, a renovated chicken coop, was destroyed in the hurricane of 1938. Its replacement was heavily damaged by Hurricane Carol in 1954 and pushed up the road by Hurricane Donna in 1960. In 1978, the business was purchased by Komes Rozes. In 1991, Flo's was washed away by Hurricane Bob, leaving only the drive-in sign. Rozes rebuilt once again, and in 1992, he opened a second location in Middletown, this time choosing a building that had already survived the 1938 hurricane. The Island Park Flo's is shown here as it looked in 2002. (CSM.)

Evelyn's Drive-In in Tiverton is named for the original owner, Evelyn DuPont, who opened the place in 1969. Back then it was just a little shack offering take-out, but later a small house was moved and added on to allow for indoor seating. In 1987, DuPont and her husband, Pat, decided to retire to Florida, and sold the business to Domenic and Jane Bitto, a young couple from near Boston. (CSM.)

Only just married the previous September, the Bittos embarked on a trial by fire, with their first weekend being the Fourth of July, one of the busiest of the year. Evelyn DuPont stayed on for two months to help them through the learning period. Overlooking picturesque Nanaquaket Pond, Evelyn's offers picnic table seating reminiscent of the old-time clambake pavilions. In 2007, Evelyn's was featured on the Food Network show *Diners, Drive-Ins and Dives*. (CSM.)

Pictured here are two late 1940s postcard views of the Fo'c's'le at Sakonnet Point in Little Compton. The Fo'c's'le was built on the ruins of the Clam House, which was destroyed in the 1938 hurricane. Its long bar served as a meeting place for fishermen, tourists, and summer folks for nearly 50 years. A year after the 1938 hurricane, the Fo'c's'le held a Fisherman's Ball, where guests dressed as fishermen paid the price of admission with a real fish. The event became an annual tradition, with music, dancing, and the telling of tall fish tales. (Both, Louis McGowan.)

The Fo'c's'le closed in 1991. Former owner Dick Rogers blamed its demise on air-conditioning: "Then . . . the malls . . . were air conditioned. So you could go to the mall, why drive down here. And of course then they got air conditioning for the house." The building stood empty and deteriorating until it was demolished in 2006, shortly after this photograph was taken. The Sakonnet Point Club was built in its place. (CSM.)

M.S. Barber's Shore Dinner House at Old Harbor on Block Island was built in 1875 and offered shore dinners for 50¢. Purchased by Henry and Alice Ballard in 1920, the business has continued under the Ballard name to the present day. The grand Ocean View Hotel burned to the ground in 1966. (PPL.)

The Ballards installed their own electric light plant in 1923 and added a third floor in 1924 and a dance hall in 1925 (shown here at the left side of the building). The hurricane of 1938 inflicted major damage—the dance hall was swept into the harbor and on the ocean side of the building the second floor collapsed—and some were sure it could not be saved, but a carpenter named Henry Rose was able to bring it back from the brink of death. The dance hall was swept into the harbor again by Hurricane Carol in 1954 but was towed in and hoisted back into place. Patrons old enough to remember this period have good memories, too—the "bluefish special," Dick Ballard counting the glasses, and Ma Ballard at the register. This postcard view is from about 1942. (CSM.)

In the late 1940s, an itinerant artist named Holden Durfee Wetherbee, in exchange for room and board, decorated the walls of the Highview Inn's bar (now known as Club Soda) with murals depicting contemporary island life. The 360-degree panorama captures nearly every prominent building of the day, including this view of Ballard's Inn. (CSM.)

This postcard view shows Ballard's around 1954, shortly before it was hit by Hurricane Carol in August and Hurricane Edna in September. Although they rebounded once again, the Ballards were evidently worn out by the experience. They sold the business to Paul C. Filippi in 1957. (DNS.)

Ballard's Inn burned to the ground on June 19, 1986 (the flames are still licking the wreckage in this photograph). The Filippi family rebuilt almost immediately, although on a slightly smaller scale, and the inn reopened the following June. Ballard's is still in business today as a combination beach resort–style hotel, restaurant, and bar. These days they sell more lobster rolls than clam cakes, but the biggest seller is their Mudslide. (Steve Filippi.)

Ernie's Old Harbor Restaurant (shown here in the 1980s) opened in 1962 in a building that had previously held C.C. Ball's General Store (1879–1928) and Block Island's post office (1928–1962). Ernie's has since become an island institution. (Fred and Debbie Howarth.)

These snapshots of Ernie's dining area are from October 1971. The occasion is a wedding breakfast for Fred and Debbie Howarth. Ernie Sherman passed away in 1974, and in 1977, the restaurant broke in two, with Ernie's focusing on breakfast upstairs, while Finn's Seafood Restaurant (named after Fred Howarth's nickname) served lunch and dinner downstairs. Both restaurants are still in business today, as is Finn's Fish Market. Fred Howarth has been setting lobster pots around Block Island for over 50 years, and the lobster bought at Finn's may be one he caught. (Both, Fred and Debbie Howarth.)

Ernie Sherman; his wife, Rita; and daughter Rosemary Howarth strike a pose behind the counter of Ernie's in 1963. The majority of the menu was breakfast and diner fare, but fried clams, oysters, scallops, fantail shrimp, fish and chips, and an oyster stew were also offered. (Ernie's Old Harbor Restaurant.)

Dead Eye Dick's at Payne's Dock, New Harbor, Block Island, has been the place to find fresh lobster since 1940. The ferry can be seen at the end of the dock at left. At Dick's Last Stand (the smaller buildings to the right of the restaurant), day-trippers could buy ice cream and rent bicycles. Dead Eye Dick's is still in business today. (CSM.)

Here is another look at Dead Eye Dick's, as seen in the 1940s Wetherbee mural at Club Soda. Before Dead Eye Dick's came on the scene, the address was the site of the New Harbor Pavilion ("Capacity 300. Shore Dinners a specialty" noted a 1904 *New York Times* advertisement), a restaurant, dance hall, and pool room owned by J.C. and C.K. Champlin. (CSM.)

A tiny clam cake shack sits amongst the hubbub of passengers embarking and disembarking the ferries at Payne's Dock in New Harbor, Block Island. The harbor was created in 1895, when, after many failed attempts and impermanent solutions, a channel was dug to connect the Great Salt Pond to the ocean. (PPL.)

Five

OTHER FISHY CONCERNS

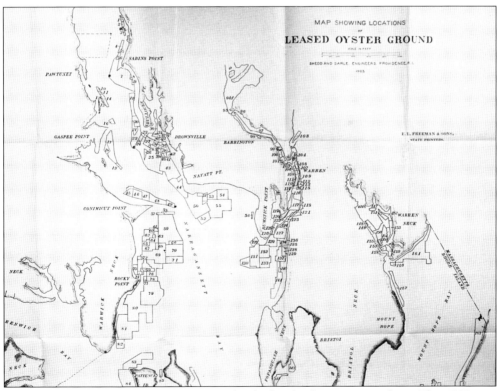

Before the quahog became synonymous with Rhode Island, oysters were king. This 1903 map of leased oyster grounds in upper Narragansett Bay shows the extent and the importance of this resource. The industry reached its height around 1912, declining afterward due to disease, pollution, a starfish population explosion, and finally the hurricane of 1938, which buried the oyster beds under layers of silt. (Richard Donnelly.)

The oyster boat *Flora*, shown here on the Barrington River fully laden with oysters, belonged to the E.M. Buckingham Oyster Company. The company, based in Drownville (West Barrington), was founded in the 1860s by brothers Jonas and Buell Buckingham. (Barrington Historical Society.)

Oysterman John Shepard (1848–1910) stands outside his Bristol oyster house in this contemporaneously retouched photograph from around 1904. That year he leased 24 acres of oyster beds in Narragansett Bay. (PPL.)

The Pettis family was big into oysters, going back generations. John Pettis ran an oyster house at 5–7 Orange Street in Providence in the 1850s; it was thought to be the very first such establishment in the city. The South Water Street address was the family's wholesale business. This envelope dates from the first decade of the 20th century. (CSM.)

Robert Pettis was said to have the largest, most succulent oysters available. A Providence newspaper reminisced that "It was the wont of Mr. Pettis to offer his patrons an oyster 'measuring seven to nine inches at the larger end' at a dollar a dozen, and the Providence gourmet who sat down to even half a dozen such knew he'd been somewhere when he rose from his seat." (PPL.)

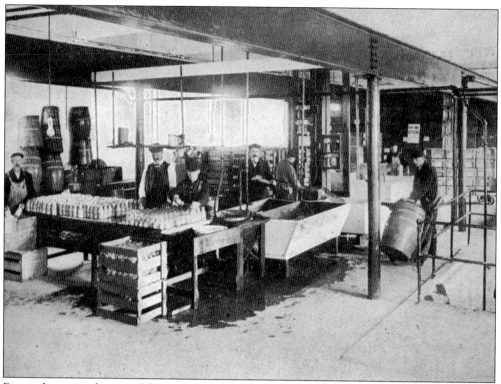

Pictured is an inside view of the American Oyster Company in Providence in 1909. The company produced Saltesea branded chowders at least through the early 1950s. The packing plant at 315 Tockwotton Street (now 258 India Street) was purchased by Brown University in 1966 and remodeled for use as a boathouse. (PPL.)

Narragansett Bay Oyster Company's warehouse and packing plant was located on Taber Avenue (now 85 Gano Street) in Providence. Note the planks laid over the oyster shell piles, which would have enabled workers to traverse the piles with wheelbarrows without getting stuck. The location is now an off-ramp from Interstate 195 West. (PPL.)

Inside Narragansett Bay Oyster Company, workers pack up product in wooden casks, barrels, and boxes. Behind the man at left are blocks of ice, to help the shellfish stay cold on its way to its destination, and a saw. According to the calendar on the wall, it is November 1908. (PPL.)

Beacon Oyster Company was founded in Wickford in 1907 by Rollin Mason and Irving Reynolds. Here, the wharf (now Pleasant Street Wharf) is being constructed. Cornelius Island, infamous in the 1860s for the persistent fragrance wafting from the Cornelius Island Fish Oil Factory, can be seen in the background across Wickford Harbor. (Tim Cranston.)

Historian Tim Cranston identifies these men as workers at either Beacon Oyster Company or Sea Coast Oyster Company, both in Wickford. Shucking oysters was cold, wet work, especially in winter, as it appears to be here. A skilled shucker can shuck an average of 16 oysters per minute. The record is 38 oysters shucked in one minute, set in 2010. (Tim Cranston.)

VISIT

New York

Quick Lunch Oyster House.

And Live Like Millionaires at Very Moderate Prices.

THOMAS F. LAHEY, Proprietor.

17 Dorrance St., Providence, R. I.

There is a lot to be said about this advertisement from the 1901 Providence City Directory. "Quick lunches" were the greasy spoons of the day, serving a mainly male clientele in dozens of spots all over the city. The tagline implies that oysters are a comestible for sophisticates (a point reinforced by the inclusion of "New York" in the business name), despite the fact that they were enjoyed by all classes at the time. (PPL.)

The fish works at Common Fence Point in Portsmouth are seen in this undated photograph. The dozens of seine boats in the foreground were used to fish for pogy (menhaden), which were processed for oil and fertilizer. The seine boats, usually carrying two men each, were towed to the fishing grounds by the tugboats docked at right. (Portsmouth Free Library/John T. Pierce Sr. Collection.)

This 1909 postcard offers a peaceful view of Poppasquash (bowdlerized here as "Pappoose Squaw") Point in Bristol, with fishermen's nets drying on the reel at left. "Remember labor day when we walked around this harbor. ha! ha! hooray," writes the correspondent. (DNS.)

Fishing Fleet, Block Island, R. I.

Fishing boats rest at anchor in Block Island's Old Harbor in this late 1800s postcard view. Block Island has no natural harbors; Old Harbor was created with stone breakwaters in 1870, and New Harbor followed in 1895 with the opening of the breachway on the west side of the Great Salt Pond. Thanks go to Keith Wahl for the following boat identifications: "To the far left, nearest the breakwater in back, there is something outfitted for harpooning sword. The boats with the point

sterns (middle and far right) are Block Island Pinkies, a design unique to B.I. that was convenient for pulling nets. In the middle, behind the two small pinkies is a genuine Banks Dory and then what appears to be a lobster smack nearest the breakwater. They all appear to be airing their sails . . . The guys in the skiff appear to be pulling a trap of some kind." (CSM.)

Apponaug Cove in Warwick was a great spot for oyster and mussels in the early 20th century, and shanties sprouted along its banks like barnacles. This postcard view of the north shore of the cove is postmarked 1911. (Judy Wilcox Jencks.)

Taken in 1957, this photograph shows the Wilcox Shanty in Apponaug and the boat *Hazel W.* belonging to Donald Wilcox and named for his wife. The shanty was rebuilt twice, after the hurricanes in 1938 and 1954. (Judy Wilcox Jencks.)

Sisters Judy and Dolores Wilcox ride the mussel dredge on the original *Hazel W.* in the 1950s. In the 1950s and 1960s, a few boats, including their father's, dredged large quantities of blue mussels and sent them to New York, but nowadays mussels are a largely overlooked species in Narragansett Bay's fisheries. (Judy Wilcox Jencks.)

This fisherman has set up shop right at the end of his rather shaky looking dock, where he appears to be cleaning fish as potential customers look on. The village of Quonochontaug is located on a neck of land between two barrier beaches in Charlestown. The image is probably from the first decade of the 20th century. (Louis McGowan.)

In its earliest days, the fish trade in Providence was conducted on floating barges rather than in shops. The schooner *Caroline*, built in 1832, was converted into such a barge in 1840 by Capt. John P. Meriam. John P. Meriam & Co. Wholesale Fish Store was located at Carpenter's Wharf below the Weybosset Bridge. Apparently still active in 1867, the barge remained at this location until it became so worm ridden and rotted that it was hauled away and broken up. (DNS.)

Four men stand in front of the Samuel Albro Fish Store in Market Square in Newport. Perhaps they are discussing an oddity that hung in Albro's store—the photograph of a tarpon that was caught in the mouth of Narragansett Bay and later bought by Albro. Before being replaced by the photograph, the tarpon itself was displayed in the fish store, until it was given to a scientist in Connecticut for study. (Providence Public Library.)

This early 1900s postcard view shows Wilcox Market at Stone Bridge in Tiverton. It was a picturesque spot to procure live lobsters, but its precarious position at the end of a dock would prove to be its undoing. (Portsmouth Free Library/John T. Pierce Sr. Collection.)

Pictured at the height of the storm, Wilcox Market at Stone Bridge in Tiverton is lashed by the wind and waves of the hurricane of 1938. The superstructure of Stone Bridge can be seen behind the market. (Portsmouth Free Library/John T. Pierce Sr. Collection.)

From 1898 to 1948, the Rhode Island Commission on Inland Fisheries operated the Lobster Hatchery on Mill Cove in Wickford, releasing 1.5 million lobsters in 1935 alone. At the hatchery, which was open to visitors, lobsters were raised from eggs before being released into the ocean once they reached the bottom-seeking stage. (Tim Cranston.)

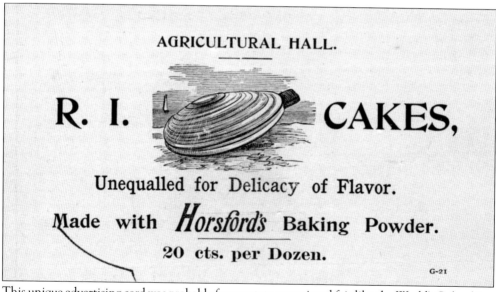

This unique advertising card was probably from a state or national fair like the World's Columbian Exposition of 1893 in Chicago, Illinois. A clam cake is a round fritter made from batter and chopped clams, then deep fried. The name of Horsford's Baking Powder, a Rhode Island product, was changed to Rumford Baking Powder in 1894, after the death of its inventor, Eben Norton Horsford. (Warwick Historical Society.)

These nifty containers holding all the fixings for a clambake could be taken home and cooked over an open fire, in a fireplace, or on a kitchen range in just an hour. The Original Wickford Clambake was a product of Wickford Shellfish Inc., a longtime fixture of Wickford with both wholesale and retail operations. (Henry A.L. Brown.)

There was a fad in the 1960s for do-it-at-home clambakes furnished by fish markets, usually packaged in tin containers. The Market By The Sea version called for adding three cups of water to the contents of lobster, clams, fish, sausage, and potatoes, then heating over a fireplace (for that rustic feeling) or a stove. This is more accurately a clam boil. (Henry A.L. Brown.)

QUONOCHONTAUG
CLAMBAKE
"The Prepared Bake That Can't Be Beat"

DIRECTIONS

Add 3 cups of water to contents, replace cover,, place on stove or over fireplace until steam rises from hole in cover. The white potato on top is your "barometer," test with fork, when potato is done your "bake" is cooked to perfection. (Usual time is one hour).

INGREDIENTS

FRESH CLAMS   LOBSTERS   FILLET FISH
SAUSAGE   WHITE POTATO   SWEET POTATO

A Complete Shore Dinner
at a Moderate Cost

We have plenty of native Lobsters, Fish, Quahogs, Little Necks, Steamers, etc., on hand at all times.

MARKET BY THE SEA

Quonochontaug Branch, Rte. 1 .   .   .   .   .   Tel. 322-0232
Weekapaug Branch, Atlantic Ave., Weekapaug   .   .   Tel. 322-7020

The Weekapaug Branch now carries cooked seafood to go.

Even restaurants were swept up in the take-home clambake fad, as shown by this advertisement from Aunt Carrie's. Aunt Carrie's made it even more of a feast by including clam cakes, chowder, and Indian pudding as add-ons. (Aunt Carrie's.)

In Rhode Island, some of the best seafood cookery happens in home kitchens and even in sailboat galleys. Ed and Sandy Rice prepared this meal of stuffed quahogs (stuffies), lobster, crab, and steamers for New Year's Eve many years ago, and the photograph has since hung in their kitchen. Ed, who loves to feed people, has also accomplished the feat of making clam cakes aboard his sailboat. The hungry cadre of friends who volunteer to help the Rices scrub and paint their boat every spring are treated to quahog chili prepared by these talented home cooks. (Ed and Sandy Rice.)

May Breakfast on May 1 is a Rhode Island tradition that began in 1867 at Oak Lawn Baptist Church in Cranston as both a celebration of spring and as a way to raise funds for a new building. In this photograph, taken on a May morning in the 1950s, church members examine a sign for one of the earliest breakfasts. Clam cakes have always been served as part of the menu at Oak Lawn's all-you-can-eat breakfast, as will be the case at the 150th breakfast on May 1, 2017. (PPL.)

Discover Thousands of Local History Books Featuring Millions of Vintage Images

Arcadia Publishing, the leading local history publisher in the United States, is committed to making history accessible and meaningful through publishing books that celebrate and preserve the heritage of America's people and places.

Find more books like this at
www.arcadiapublishing.com

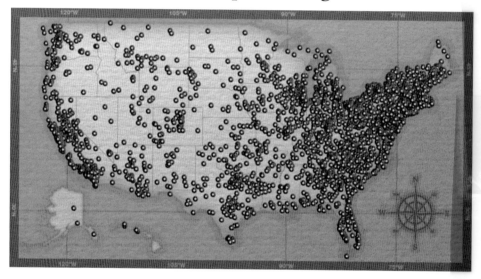

Search for your hometown history, your old stomping grounds, and even your favorite sports team.